MARVEL STUDIOS

ISBN 978-1-5400-2702-3

MARVEL SUPERHEROES MUSIC

7777 W. BLUEMOUND RD. P.O. BOX 13819 MILWAUKEE, WI 53213

In Australia Contact:
Hal Leonard Australia Pty. Ltd.
4 Lentara Court
Cheltenham, Victoria, 3192 Australia
Email: ausadmin@halleonard.com.au

Visit Hal Leonard Online at
www.halleonard.com

WAKANDA

Music by LUDWIG GÖRANSSON

Moderately

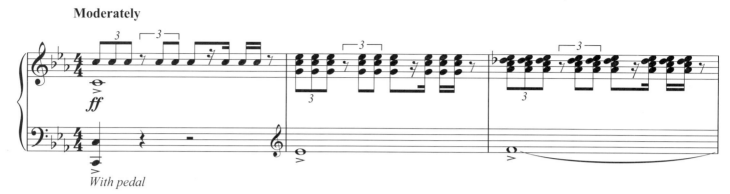

With pedal

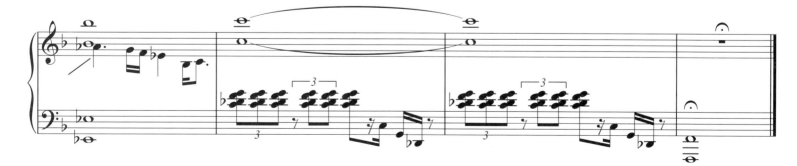

WATERFALL FIGHT

Music by LUDWIG GÖRANSSON

Moderately

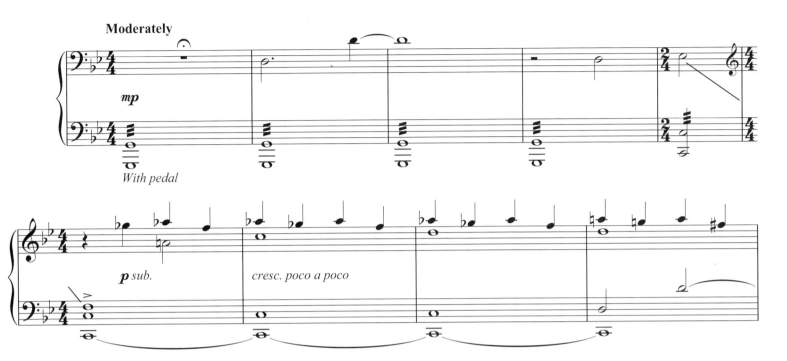

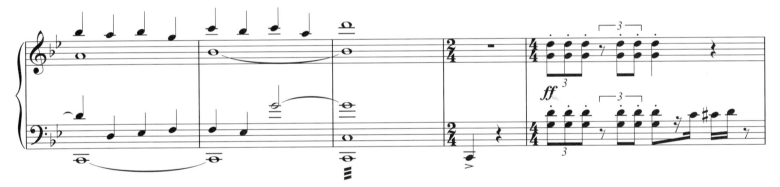

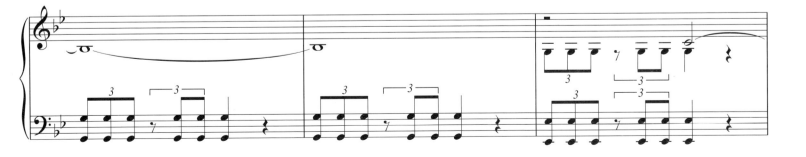

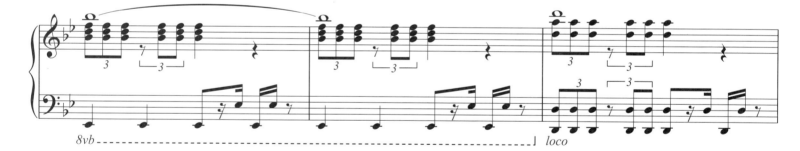

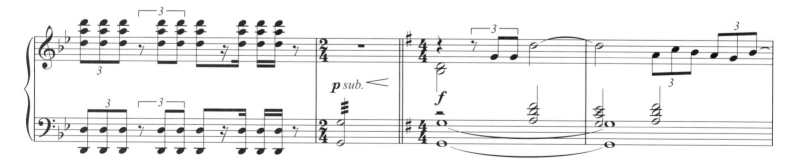

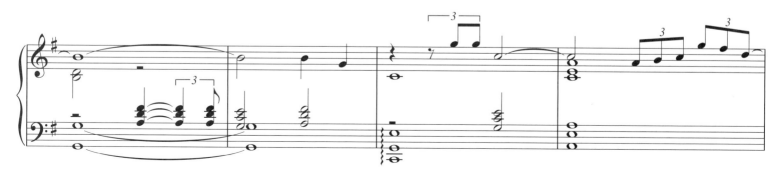

Broadly

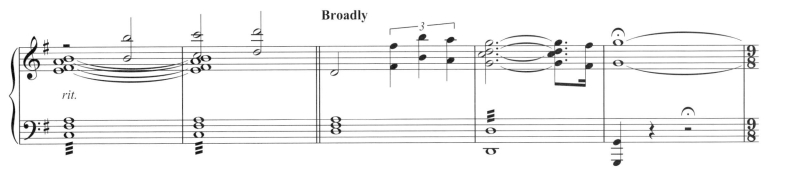

Moderately

IS THIS WAKANDA?

Music by LUDWIG GÖRANSSON

Moderately slow

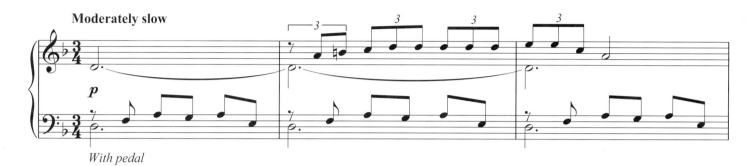

p

With pedal

cresc.

mf

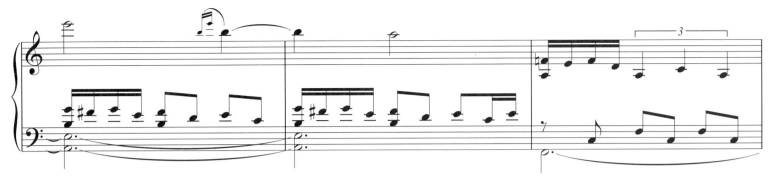

KILLMONGER VS T'CHALLA

Music by LUDWIG GÖRANSSON

Heavily (Moderately slow)

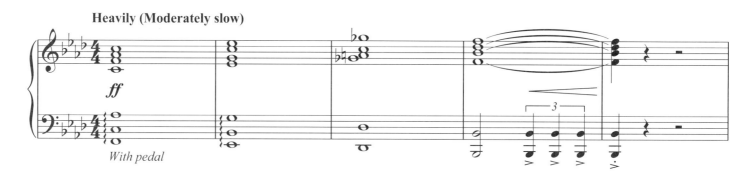

With pedal

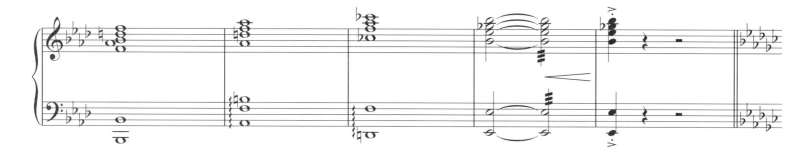

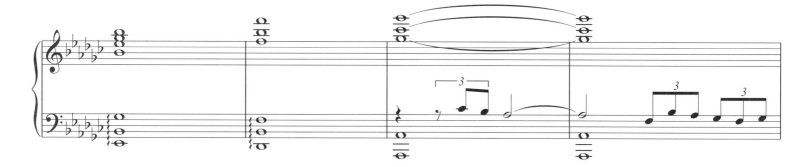

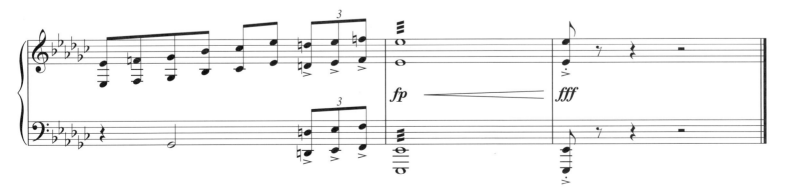

GLORY TO BAST

Music by LUDWIG GÖRANSSON

Quickly
staccato

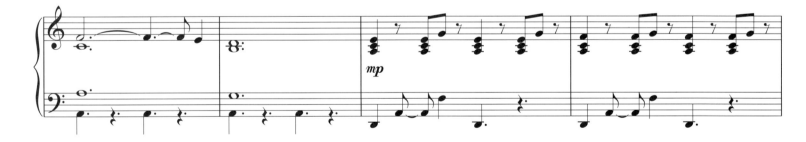

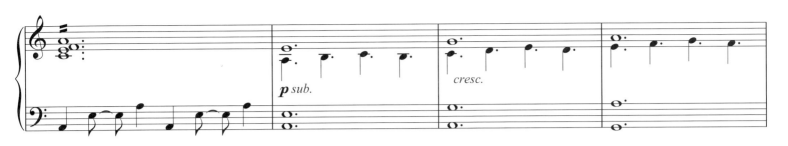

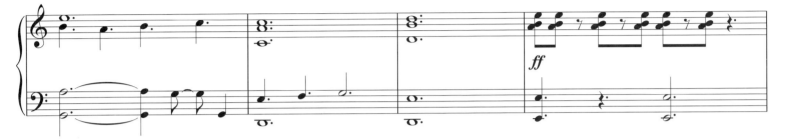

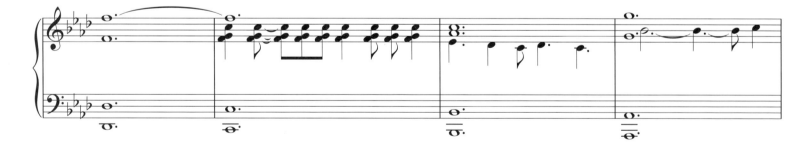

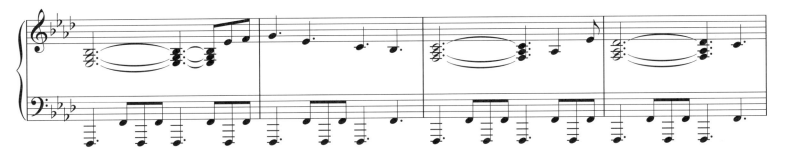

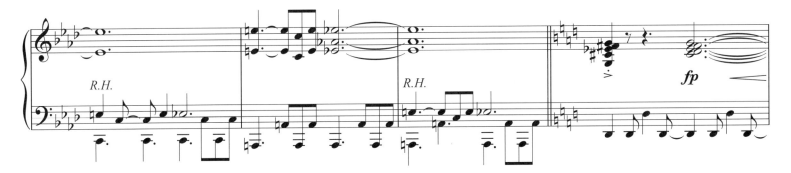

A NEW DAY

Music by LUDWIG GÖRANSSON

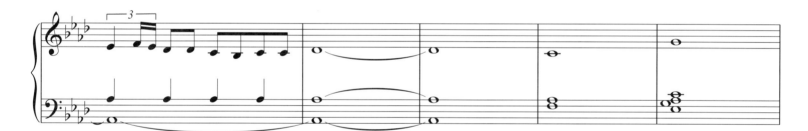

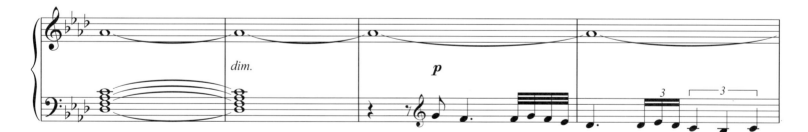

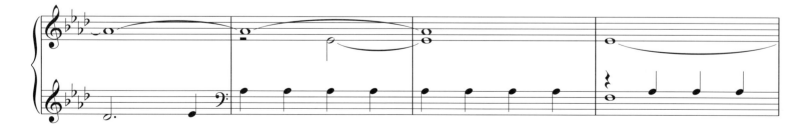

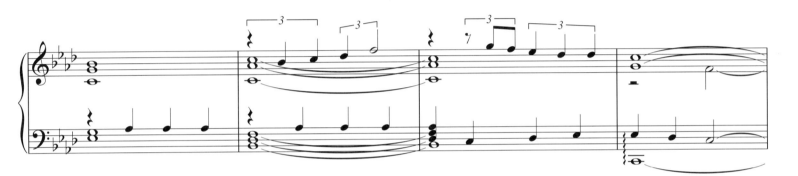

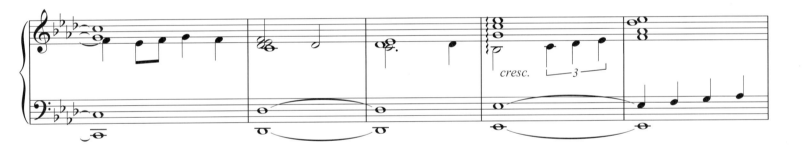

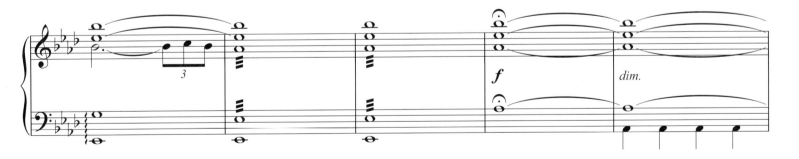

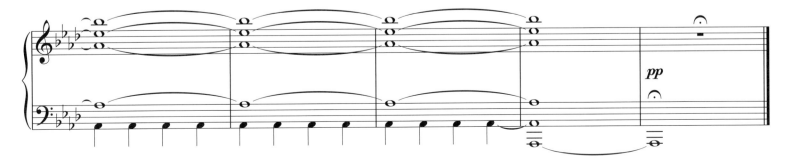

SPACESHIP BUGATTI

Music by LUDWIG GÖRANSSON

Moderately

With pedal

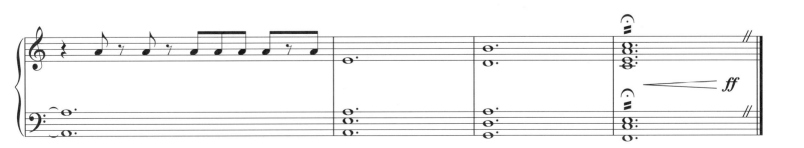

UNITED NATIONS/END TITLES

Music by LUDWIG GÖRANSSON

Very slowly

p

With pedal

mp

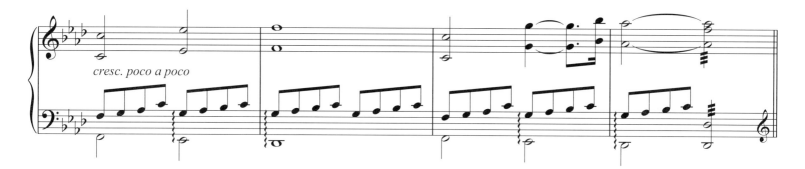

cresc. poco a poco

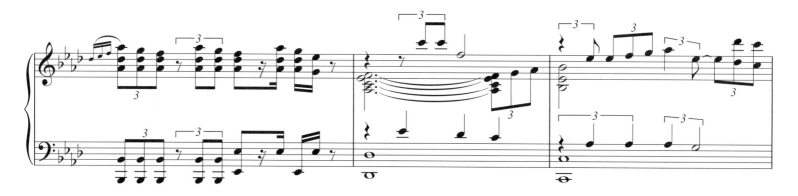

f

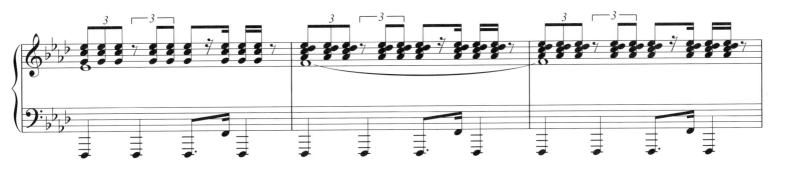

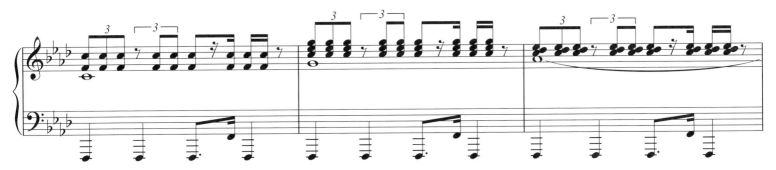

Faster

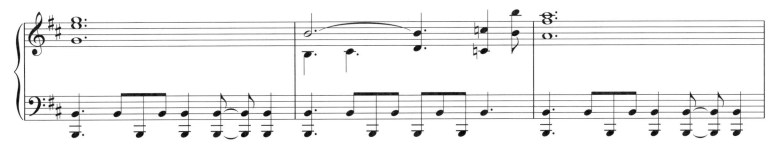

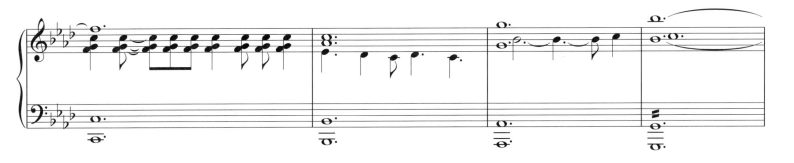

ANCESTRAL PLANE

Music by LUDWIG GÖRANSSON

Moderately

With pedal

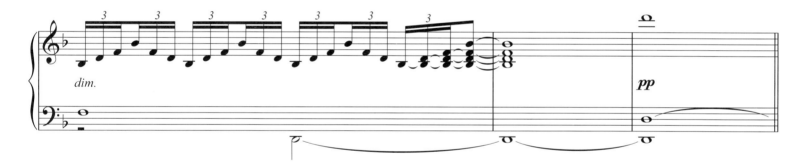

A little slower, with freedom

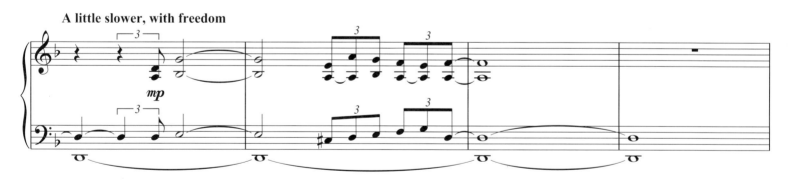

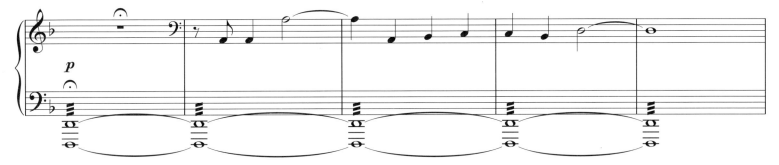

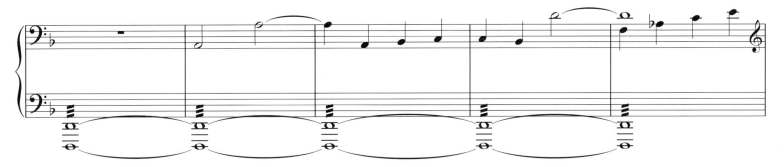

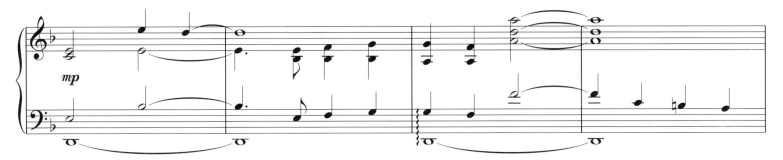

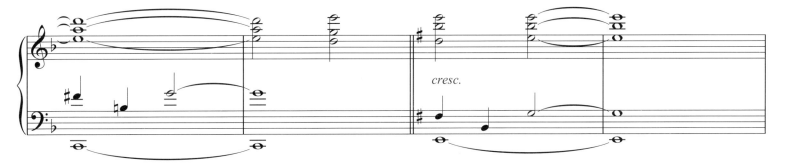

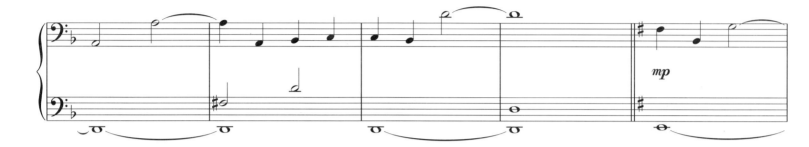

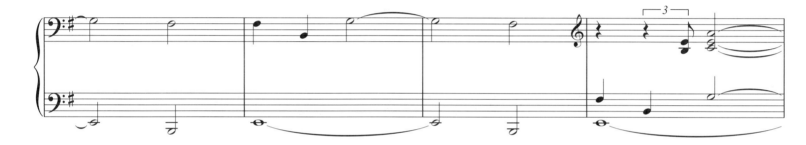